The Sacrament of Confirmation
For Confirmation Candidates

Third Edition

By ESD (Edizioni Studio Domenicano)
in collaboration with
the Institute of St. Clement I, Pope and Martyr

Preface by José Cardinal Saraiva Martins
Foreword by Archbishop John J. Myers

Illustrated by Mirko and Rosa Pellicioni

The Subcommittee on the Catechism, United States Conference of Catholic Bishops, has found this text, copyright 2013, to be in conformity with the Catechism of the Catholic Church; it may be used only as supplemental to other basal catechetical texts.

New Hope Publications

Catechism Series #3
Original Edition: ESD (Edizioni Studio Domenicano)
in collaboration with the Institute of St. Clement I, Pope and Martyr
www.istitutosanclemente.it   info@istitutosanclemente.it

Nihil Obstat:
Brian B. Reynolds, Ed.D.
Chancellor
Archdiocese of Louisville

Imprimatur:
+Joseph E. Kurtz, D.D.
Archbishop of Louisville
May 29, 2009

The *nihil obstat* and *imprimatur* are official declarations that a book or pamphlet is free of doctrinal or moral error. No implication is contained therein that those who have granted the *nihil obstat* and *imprimatur* agree with the contents, opinions, or statements expressed.

For additional copies of this book, contact:
New Hope Publications
P.O. Box 10
New Hope, KY 40052 U.S.A.
Phone: 270-325-3061   www.newhope-ky.org

ISBN 978-1-892875-51-8

Third edition, copyright 2013 New Hope Publications

We wish to acknowledge the graphic design assistance of Malb Studio Flaguel in Paris, France.

TABLE OF CONTENTS

PART THREE: WITNESSES FOR THE FAITH

This publication, *The Sacrament of Confirmation,* by Edizioni Studio Domenicano in collaboration with the Institute of St. Clement I Pope and Martyr, helps us to understand and deepen our call to perfection, our call to holiness.

The seed of holiness, which was planted in us at Baptism and at our profession of faith, requires constant nourishment so that it can mature day by day and "bear much fruit." This happens through Christian commitment, but above all through the constant help of the Spirit; indeed, we could not advance even one step along the Christian path if God did not give us His Spirit who comes to meet us, accompany us, sustain us, and crown every human effort to do good.

From the mystery of Easter, that is, from the open Heart of the crucified and glorious Redeemer, the action of grace—chiefly through the celebration of the sacraments—flows throughout history down to our own day and, through us, reaches future generations, embracing everyone in that extraordinary promise of Jesus: "Behold, I am with you all days, until the end of the world."

The sacrament of Chrismation, or Confirmation, is, *par excellence,* the "place" of Christian maturity. The gift of the Holy Spirit, who in Baptism made us children of God and brothers of Jesus, now makes us qualified witnesses to the world. God confirms His gift, and we confirm our "yes." From discipleship to the apostolate: this is the way of Christian maturity, the path of sanctity.

In this light, in the second part of this volume, the horizon expands toward a renewed reflection on the truths of the faith which, as indispensable reference points, illumine the believer's path to spiritual maturity.

The publication of this carefully-worded catechism is most opportune for helping young people (and not only young people!) toward a consciousness of the immense gift the Risen Lord gives us in Confirmation and of our consequent willingness to joyfully and freely live the values proposed to us by the Gospel.

As Prefect of the Congregation for the Causes of the Saints, I particularly value the stories of some witnesses to the faith, offered in the third part of the volume: these make us fully understand in a concrete way how it is possible to follow the path of human and Christian perfection in the various states of life.

Vatican City, Nov. 24, 2004
Jose Cardinal Saraiva Martins
Prefect of the Congregation
for the Causes of the Saints

Foreword

The Catechism of the Catholic Church (#1304) reminds us that the Sacrament of Confirmation completes Baptism and "imprints on the soul an indelible spiritual mark, the character, which is the sign that Jesus Christ has marked a Christian with the seal of His Spirit." Confirmation helps each of us to continue nurturing and developing the Lord's character and Spirit within us.

This wonderful little book, *The Sacrament of Confirmation,* clearly presents and explains to young and adult candidates alike, the many effects, virtues, gifts and fruits of this initiation Sacrament. It appropriately presents the Sacrament as being integral to our quest to live a sustained, Christian life throughout our journey here on earth. Its practical presentation, format, and many references to Sacred Scripture and the Catechism result in this book being a very effective and enjoyable catechetical tool.

Most Rev. John J. Myers
Archbishop of Newark

PART ONE

THE SACRAMENT: ITS RITES AND EFFECTS

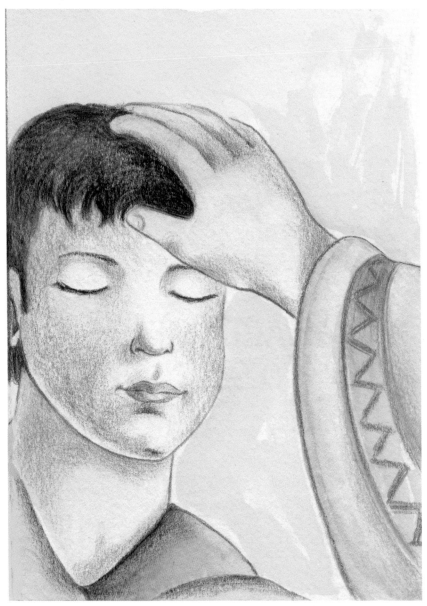

The minister of Confirmation anoints the candidate's forehead
with sacred chrism while pronouncing the words:
"Be sealed with the gift of the Holy Spirit."

What is the Sacrament of Confirmation?

1. What is Confirmation?

Confirmation, or Chrismation, is the sacrament which brings the grace of Baptism to completion through the special outpouring of the Holy Spirit. Baptism makes us Christians; Confirmation perfects us as Christians, stengthening us to be Christ's witnesses and joining us more closely with His Church. It is one of the fundamental steps along the way of Christian initiation which begins at Baptism, continues with Confirmation, and leads to the Eucharist, which is the summit of the Christian life and the goal of all the sacraments.

Confirmation, therefore, by its very nature, ought to be celebrated before the Eucharist, that is, before First Communion. However, for serious pastoral reasons, in many countries it is celebrated later in order to assure adolescents a longer religious formation.

The Eucharist, the sacrament instituted by Jesus during the Last Supper, is the goal of the journey which begins at Baptism and continues with Confirmation

2. How does Confirmation complete the grace of Baptism?

Confirmation roots us more deeply into our divine sonship and incorporates us more firmly into the life of Christ, both of which we received at Baptism. Furthermore, Vatican Council II (in *Lumen Gentium* 11) says: "By the sacrament of Confirmation [the faithful] are more perfectly bound to the Church and are endowed with the special strength of the Holy Spirit. Hence they are, as true witnesses of Christ, more strictly obliged to spread the faith by word and deed."

The Holy Spirit is at work throughout the whole world

3. Is Confirmation closely linked to the Person of the Holy Spirit?

Yes. We can better understand the significance of Confirmation if we look at it in the light of two episodes in the New Testament.

The first episode is this: after Jesus was baptized in the Jordan, He saw the Holy Spirit coming down upon Him in the form of a dove. It was only after this that Jesus began to preach the Kingdom of God (Mk 1:10).

The second instance took place when the Church was gathered in the Cenacle at Pentecost and received the Holy Spirit, who descended upon them under the form

The Baptism of Jesus in the Jordan. The dove is a symbol of the Holy Spirit

of rushing wind and tongues of fire. Only after this was the Church able to begin her mission of evangelizing the world (Acts 2:1ff).

In both cases we see the Holy Spirit completing His preceding work and giving the Church strength for her public mission.

4. Is Confirmation to the Christian what Pentecost was to the Church?

Yes. We can say that Confirmation is the "Pentecost of the Christian," among other reasons because it was on that day that Jesus instituted Confirmation. Furthermore, as we have just seen, the mission of the Church began at Pentecost, and thus the mission of the Christian, in a certain sense, also begins with the Sacrament of Confirmation. From this point of view, too, we can clearly see how Confirmation "binds us more perfectly to the Church," as Vatican Council II says in the already-cited text in question 2.

The Holy Spirit descended on Our Lady and the Apostles gathered in the Cenacle. They symbolize the whole Church which, now filled with life, could begin her mission of evangelization

5. Why is Confirmation sometimes called the sacrament of Christian maturity?

We do not say this because this sacrament must necessarily be received by adults, but because at whatever age we receive it, it strengthens us to bear courageous

The Apostles administered the Sacrament of Confirmation
by the laying on of hands

witness to our Christian faith in word and deed. This is proper to Christian maturity, though spiritual maturity does not necessarily coincide with bodily age. Young children, strengthened by the power of the Holy Spirit, have often given their lives in witness to the faith.

6. When did Jesus institute this sacrament?

After having promised this sacrament, Jesus instituted Confirmation on the day of Pentecost when He sent the Holy Spirit on the Apostles and Mary gathered in the Cenacle. The Apostles immediately began to preach and make known their faith in Jesus Christ, crucified and risen.

7. How did the Apostles confer this sacrament?

They conferred it by the laying on of hands. We read in the Acts of the Apostles (Acts 8:14-18): "Now when the apostles in Jerusalem heard that Samaria had received the word of God, they sent to them Peter and John. On their arrival they prayed for them, that they might received the Holy Spirit; for as yet he had not come upon any of them, but they had only been baptized in the name of the Lord Jesus. Then they laid their hands on them and they received the Holy Spirit."

In another passage (Acts 19:6), we read that some disciples from Ephesus were baptized, "and when Paul laid his hands on them, the Holy Spirit came upon them, and they began to speak in tongues and to prophesy."

From these texts it is evident that the Apostles were making a sacramental gesture by laying their hands on the baptized, and the effect of this gesture was the communication of the Holy Spirit.

The Sacramental Rite

8. How is the Sacrament of Confirmation conferred?

As we saw earlier, at first Confirmation was conferred by the laying on of hands; later, the anointing of the forehead with sacred chrism was added. (In the East, other sense organs are anointed as well.) As he lays his hand on the candidate and anoints the forehead with chrism, the minister (the bishop or a priest delegated by him) pronounces the words of Confirmation: "Be sealed with the gift of the Holy Spirit" (or in the East: "The seal of the gift of the Holy Spirit").

9. What is chrism?

Chrism is a mixture of olive oil and balm consecrated by the bishop on Holy Thursday. The word *Chrismation* (another name for *Confirmation*) comes from the word *chrism.*

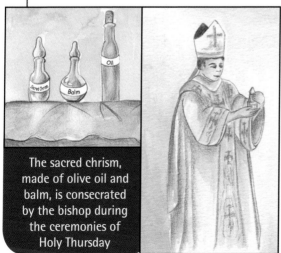

The sacred chrism, made of olive oil and balm, is consecrated by the bishop during the ceremonies of Holy Thursday

10. Why are olive oil and balm used?

Olive oil, which has the property of expanding and strengthening, signifies the grace which is infused into the soul of the Christian to confirm him in the faith. Balm, an aromatic substance which wards off corruption, shows that the Christian, strengthened by the grace of Confirmation, can practice Christian virtue and keep himself from the corruption of vice.

11. What are the words pronounced by the minister as he anoints the confirmand (person to be confirmed)?

The minister pronounces these words: "Be sealed with the gift of the Holy Spirit."

12. Why is the candidate's forehead anointed?

The candidate's forehead is anointed because the Christian is called to publicly profess his faith with his "head held high," that is, with frankness and conviction.

13. Why is the anointing done in the form of a cross?

The anointing is done in the form of a cross because the cross is the sign of the Christian. It is by the Cross of Jesus that we are saved and set free. Remember the words of the apostle St. Paul (Gal 6:14): "But as for me, God forbid that I should glory save in the cross of our Lord Jesus Christ, through whom the world is crucified to me, and I to the world."

The candidate, accompanied by his sponsor, is confirmed.
The minister anoints his or her forehead with sacred chrism
in the form of a cross and sends him or her
to be a witness for the faith

The Effects of Confirmation

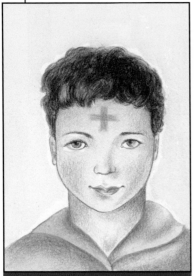

The character of a perfect Christian, received in Confirmation, is like an indelible mark on the heart of the confirmed Christian

14. What are the effects of Confirmation?

As we know, the sacraments communicate grace, that is, friendship with God. The grace of Confirmation, besides rooting us more deeply in our divine sonship, uniting us more firmly to Christ and making our bond with the Church more perfect, also gives us the strength to witness to our faith before the world without embarrassment, but rather with enthusiasm and joy.

15. Does Confirmation also confer the seven gifts of the Holy Spirit?

Since grace is always accompanied by the gifts of the Holy Spirit, all the sacraments, while giving us grace, also increase the gifts of the Holy Spirit in us. In Confirmation, however, the gifts take on a special significance because this sacrament confers the Holy Spirit in His fullness (see question #2).

16. What are the seven gifts of the Holy Spirit?

The gifts of the Holy Spirit are supernatural qualities or special capacities God gives us to enable us to be more docile in following His inspirations to do good. While the virtues make us docile in accepting the commands of right reason illumined by faith, the gifts make us docile in receiving the inspirations of God Himself. We attribute these inspirations to the Person of the Holy Spirit.

The virtues are like oars which propel the boat forward with great effort; the gifts of the Spirit are like sails which push the boat forward without any effort on the part of the rowers

The virtues can be compared to oars which move the boat forward by dint of hard work and on the initiative of the rower, while the gifts can be compared to sails which, when the wind blows, propel the boat forward

The girl on the left received Confirmation and wants to follow Jesus. The other youth, instead, distances himself from Jesus because, either by choice or through carelessness, he refuses to become a "true witness" for Christ

without any effort or initiative on the part of the rower, but only on the part of the wind.

17. What are the names of the seven gifts of the Holy Spirit?

The seven gifts of the Holy Spirit are wisdom, understanding, counsel, fortitude, knowledge, piety, and fear of the Lord.

18. What is the characteristic of each of these gifts?

Wisdom gives us a taste for divine things. Understanding helps us understand the truths of the faith more deeply. Counsel suggests the right way to act in unforeseen and difficult situations. Fortitude gives us strength to withstand the greatest trials, even martyrdom. Knowledge helps us discover the divine wisdom and power in creatures. Piety makes us feel in the depths of our souls that God is our Father. Fear of the Lord gives us respect and reverence towards God and sacred things.

19. Does Confirmation imprint a character?

Yes, Confirmation does imprint a character or an indelible sign. Just as Baptism imposes a character which remains forever and can never be lost in any way, so too, Confirmation imprints its own character which can never be lost. For this reason, Confirmation can only be received once in a person's life.

20. What are the characteristics of the character received in Confirmation?

The character, which distinguishes the confirmed from those not confirmed, incorporates us into Christ in a perfect manner. In other words, the character molds the soul, conforming it to Christ the prophet, priest and king. This conforming was begun in Baptism, but Confirmation strengthens it, especially in the area of prophecy, or giving witness.

21. What does it mean to be conformed to Christ the prophet, priest and king?

To be conformed to Christ the prophet, priest and king means to imitate Him:

—as *prophet* by witnessing to the truth of our faith;

The letter L (Love) indelibly impressed on the heart of the confirmed Christian

—as *priest* by giving due worship to God by prayers of praise, petition and intercession; and offering ourselves to God in the Sacrifice of the Mass

—as *king* by exercising the lordship of reason over our own actions, in order to accomplish good and avoid evil.

The Conferral of the Sacrament

22. Who can receive Confirmation?

Any baptized person who has not yet been confirmed can receive Confirmation.

23. What are the conditions for receiving Confirmation worthily?

To receive Confirmation worthily one must be baptized and must be in the state of grace. If the candidate has reached the age of reason, he or she must have the intention of receiving the sacrament and must also be prepared to take on the role of Christ's disciple and to bear witness to Him both within the Church and in temporal affairs.

To receive Confirmation worthily one must first make a good confession to obtain pardon of his sins

24. What would happen if a person received Confirmation while he was not in the state of grace?

While such a person would receive the *character* of Confirmation, he would not obtain any spiritual benefit, and he would commit a sacrilege because he would be violating the sacredness of the sacrament. To receive the particular grace of Confirmation, he would have to seek forgiveness of his sins in confession.

25. Can Confirmation be received even by babies before they have the use of reason?

Yes. In fact, the Church recommends that if a baby is in danger of death, he should receive Confirmation as well as Baptism.

26. Who can administer Confirmation?

The minister of Confirmation is the Bishop. Since Confirmation is a sacrament leading to perfection, it is logical and fitting that it be administered by one who possesses the fullness and perfection of the priesthood, the Bishop. For practical motives, however, the Bishop can delegate a priest to administer Confirmation; but in these cases it is necessary that the chrism used should have been consecrated by the Bishop.

27. Why does the candidate have a sponsor?

The candidate has a sponsor because it is appropriate and helpful for the parents, who are the first educators in the faith, to be assisted by committed Christians who act as "teachers," helping and guiding their children in

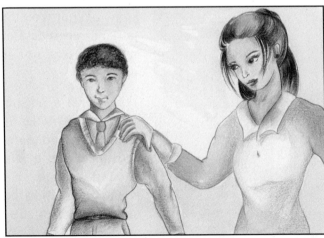

The sponsor has the important task of helping parents guide their children on their journey of faith

witnessing to the faith and carrying out the practices of Christian life. It is fitting that the sponsor be one of the candidate's godparents, since the sacraments of Baptism and Confirmation are so closely linked.

28. Is Confirmation an important sacrament?

Since all the sacraments were instituted by Jesus Christ, each one by its nature is important. Confirmation has taken on a particular importance in our time because large segments of society are distancing themselves from the faith. For this reason a new evangelization is needed. The Sacrament of Confirmation fills this very need: that all may be apostles of the truth and of God's love, witnesses for Jesus Christ, the only Savior of the world.

> In some countries, including the United States, the confirmand may take a Confirmation name, choosing a saint with whom he or she feels a special affinity and whose virtues he or she wishes to imitate. By taking the saint's name, the confirmand asks this saint to be a helper and guide as he or she seeks to live the Christian life more fully and courageously through the Sacrament of Confirmation.

PART TWO

THE TRUTHS OF THE CATHOLIC FAITH

The "handing over" of the Creed *(Traditio Symboli)* takes place first in the baptismal rite, because the beginning of salvation comes about through faith and Baptism. But "the faith required for Baptism is not a perfect and mature faith, but a beginning that is called to develop.... For all the baptized, children or adults, faith must grow *after* Baptism."
(Catechism of the Catholic Church, 1253 and 1254)

We will now offer a brief commentary on the Creed which is recited at Mass, so that preparation for the Sacrament of Confirmation, which gives us the strength to be witnesses for our faith, might become a means and occasion to know that faith better and more deeply.

The main truths of the Catholic faith
are found in the Creed

The Creed

29. Where do we find the chief truths of the faith which the Christian—in particular, one who is being confirmed—must believe and to which he must bear witness?

These truths are found in the Creed, which is also called a Symbol.

30. Do we have only one version of the Creed?

No, we have several versions. The oldest is what is called the *Symbol of the Apostles;* the best known, called the *Nicene-Constantinopolitan Creed,* is the one we recite during Sunday Mass.

31. Why do we call it the Nicene-Constantinopolitan Creed?

We call it the *Nicene-Constantinopolitan Creed* because it was formulated by the Council of Nicea (AD 325) and by the Council of Constantinople (AD 381). Here is the official text in English:

I believe in one God,
the Father almighty,
maker of heaven and earth,
of all things visible and invisible.

I believe in one Lord Jesus Christ,
the Only Begotten Son of God,
born of the Father before all ages.
God from God, Light from Light,
true God from true God
begotten, not made, consubstantial with the Father:
through him all things were made.
For us men and for our salvation
he came down from heaven,
and by the Holy Spirit was incarnate of the Virgin Mary,
and became man.

For our sake he was crucified under Pontius Pilate,
he suffered death and was buried,
and rose again on the third day
in accordance with the Scriptures.
He ascended into heaven
and is seated at the right hand of the Father.
He will come again in glory
to judge the living and the dead
and his kingdom will have no end.

I believe in the Holy Spirit, the Lord, the giver of life,
who proceeds from the Father and the Son,
who with the Father and the Son is adored and glorified,
who has spoken through the prophets.

I believe in one, holy, catholic and apostolic Church.
I confess one Baptism for the forgiveness of sins
and I look forward to the resurrection of the dead
and the life of the world to come. Amen.

Now we will attempt to deepen our understanding of each article of the Creed.

I Believe in One God

32. What do the words "I believe" signify?

They signify: "I hold this as certain, as more certain than if I were seeing it with my own eyes."

33. Where does this certainty come from?

This certainty comes from the fact that these truths have been revealed by God. He is infallible Truth, who can neither deceive nor be deceived. There is nothing more certain than the truths revealed by God.

34. What is the first truth we believe?

The first truth we believe is that there is only one God, only one Being who is pure spirit, Truth and Love, who is all-perfect, infinite and omnipotent (all-powerful), who has existed necessarily from all eternity and on whom all things depend. He Himself revealed His name, which expresses His nature: "I am who am" (Ex 3:14).

35. Is faith the only way to know that God exists?

No, we know that God exists not only because faith teaches us so, but also because reason proves this truth.

The light of the One True God illumines the world

How can our reason prove the existence of God?

Our reason can prove the existence of God by reasoning from effect to cause. For example, when we see smoke, we can reason to the existence of a fire.

However, to prove the existence of God with certainty, human reason must be formed and educated, just as a doctor who wants to do his work well must be well educated.

St. Thomas Aquinas presents several ways reason can prove God's existence. Here is one of them:

"Some things lacking reason, such as natural bodies, act for an end, as we can see from the fact that they act always or nearly always in the same way in order to reach perfection. From this it appears that they reach their end not by chance, but by a predisposition. Now, that which is lacking intelligence does not tend toward an end unless it is directed by a knowing and intelligent being, as in the case of an arrow shot by the archer. Thus there must be some intelligent being by whom all natural things are ordered to an end; and this being we call God."

Another convincing way to perceive God, in addition to rational proofs, is the emotive and poetic way, so

23

well expressed, for example, by these words of the poet Metastasius: "Wherever I look, I see you, O immense God; I admire you in your works; I recognize you in myself."

37. Can human reason tell us other things about God besides proving His existence?

Yes, reason, with much study and application, can also prove that God is a pure spirit, that He is one and eternal, that He is infinite goodness and truth, and that all things depend on Him. Two great philosophers, Plato and Aristotle, came to understand without the aid of Sacred Scripture that God has these perfections.

38. What does the expression "pure spirit" mean?

The expression "pure spirit" means that God is not composed of spirit and matter as we are, but that He is spirit alone. What is material can be seen, touched, measured, etc. The spirit, on the other hand, cannot be apprehended by our senses, even if the intellect shows its existence. This is true of the human soul as well, which is a spiritual reality. Our senses cannot see it or touch it, but it is certainly the principle which gives life to our body, and is also the principle of our thoughts, choices, loving, etc.

39. So there is only one God, all-perfect, infinite and eternal. The Catholic faith, however, affirms that God is one but also three: the Father, the Son and the Holy Spirit.

Yes, our faith teaches us that the one God exists in three Persons equal and distinct: Father, Son and Holy Spirit. However, this trinity of Persons does not detract from the oneness of God. In fact, all three–the Father, the Son and the Holy Spirit–are one God. This is the principal mystery of our faith, which we remember every time we make the sign of the cross, saying, "In the name of the Father and of the Son and of the Holy Spirit." But this mystery of the Blessed Trinity will be better explained when we examine the parts of the Creed concerning the Son and the Holy Spirit (questions 58-61 and 95-99).

40. What do we call those who deny the existence of God?

Those who deny the existence of God are called atheists. Atheism goes against reason and faith. The Bible says that the man who says God does not exist is a fool (Ps 13:1).

God is one, but also triune—that is, He exists in three equal and distinct Persons: the Father, the Son, and the Holy Spirit

The Father Almighty

41. Why do we say that God is Father?

We say this in a general sense to indicate that God is infinitely good and also that He is the primary source of all things. However, the word *Father* refers first and foremost to the mystery of the Blessed Trinity, which signifies that God is the Father of the Eternal Son whom He begets from all eternity. In the second place this word indicates that God, through the grace of Baptism, has called us to be His adopted children (Eph 1:5), and therefore to be, in a certain sense, brothers of Jesus Christ, His only Son. In the third place this word reminds us that God cares for all His creatures as a father cares for his children.

42. What does the word "almighty" signify?

It signifies that God is omnipotent or infinite in power, because "nothing is impossible with God" (Lk 1:37). He is omnipotent above all in forgiving.

God is the Father of the whole human race

43. Can God do evil?

No, God cannot do evil, because He is infinite goodness. He cannot do evil because He cannot will to do so, since evil is the opposite of good—or, in other words, evil is the contrary of the divine essence.

44. But if everything depends on God, and God cannot will evil, why does evil exist?

There are two types of evil: moral evil, or sin, and physical-material evil, which means some evil in our body or in the world around us. Moral evil, or sin, originates only in our bad choices, which God tolerates in order to leave us free; physical or material evil, however, is either the consequence of sin, or else comes from the laws of nature which perfects itself by transforming things, as when the grain of wheat dies in order to produce fruit.

45. How can sin be the source of physical or material evil?

Sin can be the source of physical or material evil as a consequence of individual sin, that is, of individual persons' sins, as when one person does something evil to another (stealing, calumniating, treating another unjustly, etc.) or when one hurts himself, damaging his own body through vices. But physical or material evil is also the consequence of original sin (question #56) which disturbed the order of creation, introducing fatigue, suffering, sickness and death into our lives.

46. How do God's goodness and almighty power manifest themselves?

They manifest themselves above all in creation (this is why we say that God is the creator and that He created all things with the love of a father), and in the

Redemption, of which the Creed speaks farther on, after having affirmed the Incarnation of the Son for our salvation.

St. Augustine expresses another characteristic of the goodness and divine power in these words: "God, being supremely good, would in no way permit any evil among His works unless He were powerful enough and good enough to bring good even out of evil." It is God's very goodness which permits evil from which He can then bring good.

God's permissive will is a mystery which we cannot fully understand, but it is His very goodness which permits evil from which He can then bring good. Witness the power of good triumphing over evil in the Passion and Death of Christ. God permitted this greatest of all evils and by it brought about the redemption of the whole human race.

Maker of Heaven and Earth, of All Things Visible and Invisible

47. What does it mean to say that God is the Creator?

To say that God is the Creator means that God made all things from nothing and keeps them in existence by His Providence. God creates with wisdom and love: "Creation is the foundation of 'all God's saving plans,' the 'beginning of the history of salvation' that culminates in Christ" (CCC 280).

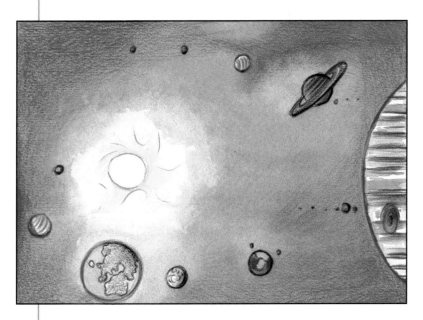

God is the creator of all things visible and invisible,
from the greatest to the least

48. What does the expression "of heaven and earth" mean?

God created minerals, plants, animals and human beings, but also invisible realities like angels

It means that God is the Creator of all that exists (except for Himself), whether spiritual or material, as the words immediately following that phrase explain: "of all things visible and invisible."

49. Are there, then, other invisible realities besides God, who, as we have said, is pure spirit?

Yes, there are spiritual creatures which are invisible to human eyes—angels and also human souls. God creates a human soul every time a baby is conceived.

50. What is the difference between the angels and the human soul?

The angels are pure spirits, created to exist without bodies, while human souls were created to be united with bodies, even though they do exist separately from the body after death, in expectation of the Resurrection (questions 113-115). Both angels and human souls are immortal.

51. What do we know about the angels?

We know that angels are spiritual creatures gifted with intelligence and free will. Sacred Scripture speaks very frequently about the angels. They are much more perfect and powerful than we are. They are part of God's plan for salvation. The Church, too, benefits from the mysterious and powerful help of the angels.

We should constantly recommend ourselves to the good angels, especially our guardian angels

Some angels remained faithful to God, who had called them to a very particular friendship with Him through the gift of divine grace, and they were allowed to enter Paradise. These are the good angels who watch over us and protect us.

Some of the angels, however, rebelled against God and refused His grace; these angels are called demons, and they have been condemned to Hell forever. They try to lead us away from God.

We should constantly recommend ourselves to our good angels, above all to our guardian angels, and keep ourselves from the snares of the devil, who wants to tempt us to do evil.

Some of the angels remained faithful to God; others rebelled and were condemned to Hell. These are the demons, who try to lead us away from God

52. Which is the noblest of all God's visible creatures?

The noblest of God's visible creatures is the human person, created in the image of God and able to know and love his own Creator. It is true that the human person belongs to the material world on account of his body, but it is also true that he is like the angels because of his spiritual and immortal soul.

53. How did God create the human person?

"Male and female He created them." Man and woman were willed by God for each other. Both are made in the image of God.

54. Does the human person have free will?

Yes, because of his spiritual soul the human person is master of his actions, and can choose one thing rather than another, such as doing good rather than doing evil.

55. What are the consequences of this freedom?

The consequences of this freedom are: a person can deliberately oppose God's will and refuse His love, separating himself from God; but he is also able to return God's love by living in His friendship.

56. How did man, who had been newly created by God, use this freedom?

Man was called, like the angels, to a very special friendship with God; but he allowed himself to be seduced by the devil and he disobeyed God. Because of this he lost, both for himself and for all his descendants, the gifts that God had given him, and he became subject to suffering, death and the tyranny of the passions, which war against the soul.

Today humanity, on account of the sin of our first parents, finds itself in a condition of opposition and disobedience to God, a condition from which we cannot save ourselves by our own powers. This situation of sin is called "original sin." Every person, from the moment of his conception, bears this inherited burden from which, as we shall see, only Jesus Christ can save us, reopening for us the gates of Paradise and calling each one to become an adopted child of God.

Adam and Eve allowed the devil to tempt them, and they disobeyed God.
For this they were cast out of the Garden of Paradise

Jesus, born of the Virgin Mary, is the Only-begotten Son of the Father

I believe in one Lord Jesus Christ, the Only Begotten Son of God, eternally begotten of the Father before all ages. God from God, Light from Light, true God from true God, begotten, not made, consubstantial with the Father; through Him all things were made.

57. Why is this part of the Creed which concerns the Person of Jesus Christ so extensive?

It is lengthy because this Creed, or symbol, was drawn up at the Council of Nicea (A.D. 325) to condemn the heresy of Arius (256-336), who denied the divinity of Jesus Christ, the fundamental truth of the Christian faith.

58. Why is the divinity of Jesus Christ the fundamental truth of the Christian faith?

Since Jesus Christ is true God, He is therefore also the true Savior who offers us friendship with God and eternal life (cf. Catechism of the Catholic Church, 1). The Christian faith corresponds to the declaration of St. Peter, the first among the Apostles, who said, "You are the Christ, the Son of the living God" (Mt 16:16), and also to the testimony of Thomas the Apostle: "My Lord and my God" (Jn 20:28).

Therefore Jesus Christ is the Son of God, or the Word; He is the second Person of the Blessed Trinity. He is God, like the Father, by His very nature or substance, as Jesus Himself affirms: "I and the Father are one" (Jn 10:30). He is uncreated, otherwise He would not be God (He would be a creature, as Arius held), but He is generated. The name "Jesus" indicates that He is the Savior, and the name "Christ" (which signifies *anointed,* or *consecrated)* signifies that He is the promised Messiah.

59. If, however, the Word was begotten, it would seem that He must have had a beginning.

No, this is not the case. In fact the Word, or the Son, was generated from all eternity and in eternity. Therefore He proceeds from the Father by generation, but He proceeds eternally, and thus there was never a time when He was not.

60. Can you explain this point further?

Here is an example. If the sun had existed from all eternity, its rays would have shone eternally and would never have *begun* to shine. And yet the rays *proceed from,* or *come from* the sun; we could almost say that they are *generated by* the sun.

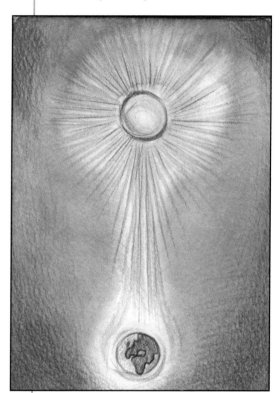

The Word proceeds from the Father like rays proceed from the sun

In the same way, we can say that the Word issues forth from the Father just as radiance comes from light. If the light is eternal, its radiance is also eternal.

61. In what way can we speak of generation in God?

Western theology, mostly thanks to St. Augustine and St. Thomas Aquinas, sought to explain this mystery by saying that the Word proceeds from the mind of the Father like a most perfect idea the Father has of Himself, of His own divine nature. This idea is a perfect reproduction of the Father, absolutely identical to the Father, and, being a pure spirit like the Father, is also of the same nature or substance as the Father. God is pure spirit, and the idea He has of Himself is also pure spirit. The idea is consubstantial with Him. Since, however, this idea proceeds from the Father, or comes from the Father, we say it is generated. Because God is pure spirit, we can say that the idea He has of Himself is generated by Him, since it is consubstantial with Him.

62. Why do we say that "through Him all things were made"?

We say this because the Word, being God just as the Father is, is also the Creator just as the Father is.

> For us men and for our salvation, He came down from Heaven, and by the Holy Spirit was incarnate of the Virgin Mary, and became man

63. What is the salvation which Jesus came to bring us?

Jesus came to bring us salvation from sin and its consequences: suffering and death. Together with this salvation we receive the call to become adoptive children and friends of God. "No longer do I call you servants...but I have called you friends, because I have made known to you all that I have heard from my Father" (Jn 15:15).

64. Is there any other savior besides Jesus?

No. Jesus is the only Savior, as St. Peter clearly affirms: "Neither is there salvation in any other. For there is no other name under heaven given to men by which we must be saved" (Acts 4:12).

65. How did Jesus save us from sin?

Jesus saved us from sin through the gift of grace which sanctifies the soul, wiping out original sin and those sins which separate us from God, that is, mortal sins.

The gift of grace sanctifies our souls, wiping out original sin and making us adopted children of God

66. So grace does more than wipe out our sins?

Yes. Grace, which is friendship with God, also makes us adopted children of God, participants in his own divine life and able (after death) to see God. This will be the eternal beatitude or happiness of Paradise.

67. How does Jesus save us from suffering and death?

Jesus has made it possible in this life for suffering and death, if accepted with love, to become instruments of salvation for ourselves and others; in the life to come He has made it possible for us to be totally freed from suffering and death through the resurrection.

68. If the Eternal Word "came down from Heaven," does this mean that He left Heaven?

No. The Word, the Eternal Son of God, did not and does not leave Heaven, but is always "in the bosom of the Father," as the Gospel says (Jn 1:18).

69. In what way did the Word come down from Heaven?

The Word, being God, was already present not only in Heaven, but also on earth and everywhere. However, at the Incarnation He made Himself present on this earth in a new way, in Jesus' humanity. In this sense the Word was sent by the Father (cf. Gal 4:4), and came to live amongst us (cf. Jn 1:14).

70. What do we mean by saying that the Word became flesh?

We mean that He assumed or took on human nature. The second Person of the Blessed Trinity, the Eternal Word, generated by the Father before all ages, at a certain moment in human history, "in the fullness of time" (Gal 4:4), without giving up His divine nature which He possesses from eternity, made human nature His own; that is, He united to Himself a very particular human nature so as to form only one Person. Thus the eternal Word, after the Incarnation, had two natures, a divine nature and a human nature. The first He possessed from all eternity; the second He acquired in time.

71. Is this mystery important?

This mystery of the Incarnation is one of the core mysteries of our faith, and it is formulated in a manner corresponding to the central mystery of the Trinity. In fact, the mystery of the Trinity was formulated thus: three distinct Persons and only one nature; while that of the Incarnation is formulated this way: one Person and two distinct natures.

The importance of this mystery is also emphasized when at these words of the Mass: "by the Holy Spirit...[He] became man," the Church prescribes that we bow as a sign of adoration. A confirmed Christian should not omit this witness to his faith.

72. How did Jesus' conception take place?

Jesus' conception took place in a miraculous manner through the work of the Holy Spirit. The Virgin Mary, whom God had chosen to be the Mother of Jesus, conceived Him by the Holy Spirit without the help of a man. And the Virgin Mary, on account of the infinite dignity of her Son, always preserved her virginity. She is the ever-Virgin.

73. What does the expression "Mother of God" mean in reference to the Virgin Mary?

This expression does not signify that she generated the divinity, but rather that she gave a human nature to the Eternal Word, who is true God. Since she is the mother of the one Person who is Jesus Christ, true God and true man, she is also the Mother of God.

74. Has God revealed to us any other truths about the Mother of Jesus?

Yes. Beyond Mary's divine maternity and perpetual virginity, God has also revealed her Immaculate Conception. This means that Mary, in view of the merits of

The Virgin Mary gave Jesus, Who is God, His human nature; therefore she is Mother of God

her Son, was preserved from original sin, which every human being inherits from the moment of conception. God also revealed her Assumption into heaven. This means that the Blessed Mother is already in Paradise with her body as well as her soul, while everyone else must wait for the final resurrection for their bodies to enter heaven (see question n. 113).

The Blessed Virgin, through the merits of her Son, was preserved from original sin and assumed bodily into Heaven, while the rest of us must wait for the resurrection of the dead for our bodies to enter Heaven

For our sake
He was crucified
under Pontius Pilate;
He suffered death and was buried

75. How can one express the mystery of the Incarnation in a few words?

One can express it this way: Jesus is true God and true man. And we notice that the expression "Mother of God" perfectly sums up these truths: in fact, if Mary is Mother *of God*, this shows that Jesus is true God; if Mary is *Mother* of God, this shows that Jesus is truly man (otherwise Mary could not be his true mother).

76. How did Jesus save us?

Jesus saved us through the Paschal Mystery of His Passion and Death on the Cross, His Resurrection from the dead, and His Ascension into Heaven.

77. In what sense did His Death on the Cross save us?

This is a profound mystery, but great theologians of the past have explained it this way: since sin is an offense against God, who is an infinite Being, every sin has an infinite dimension. Thus there was need of expiation, or redemption, of infinite value in order to make up for it. No merely human person, no matter how holy, could offer this reparation. Only Jesus, true God and true man, was able to offer the Father infinite reparation in our place, to pay back the infinite offense of sin. The sacrifice of Jesus on the Cross is made present on the altar every time Holy Mass is celebrated.

78. Was it necessary for Jesus to suffer that much?

No, in itself it was not necessary, because even the smallest of His sufferings, since it was the suffering of a divine Person, had an infinite value. But Jesus wanted to suffer the whole Passion and the cruel death of the Cross to help us understand the evil of sin and the immensity of His love for us.

79. What does it mean to say that Jesus died?

To say that Jesus died means the same as it would mean for any man: that the soul separated from the body. However, since the human nature of Jesus is united to the divinity, one might ask what happened to the body and soul of Jesus after death. The answer is that His soul and body, though they were separated from each other, remained united to His divinity. The body of Jesus, united to the Eternal Word, was placed in the tomb, and the soul of Jesus, united to the Eternal Word, descended to the lower regions to free the souls of the just of the Old Testament (cf. 1 Pt 3:19).

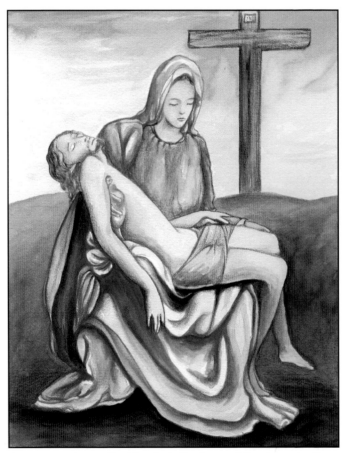

Jesus wanted to suffer His whole Passion and Death on the Cross
to help us understand how immense is His love for us

And rose again
on the third day
in accordance
with the Scriptures

80. What does it mean to say that Jesus rose from the dead?

This means that Jesus' soul was reunited with His body. However, after the Resurrection Jesus' body would have new properties in addition to those He had had before His Death on the Cross. Before His Death His body was passible (able to suffer) and mortal; after His Resurrection His body would be glorious, impassible and immortal.

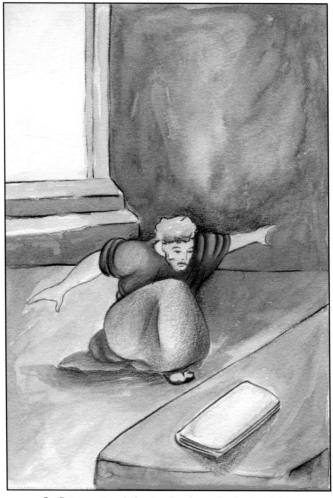

St. Peter entered the tomb where the body of Jesus had been laid, and found it empty

81. How do we know that Jesus rose from the dead?

We know that Jesus rose from the dead because the tomb where His body had been laid was found empty. Another proof is that the risen Jesus appeared, first to the women, and then repeatedly to the Apostles, who at first doubted, as the Gospels clearly tell us.

The Resurrection of Jesus is both an historical fact and a mystery of faith. As an historical fact it is a miracle which proves the truth of our faith. As a mystery it introduces us to God's plan, in which the Risen Jesus was the first-born of the new world, of that "world to come" which we mention at the end of the Creed.

82. Is the Resurrection of Jesus an important event?

The Resurrection of Jesus is an event of prime importance, so much so that the Apostle St. Paul even says that if Christ was not raised, "vain then is our preaching, vain too is your faith" (1 Cor 15:14).

83. Why do we say "in fulfillment of the Scriptures"?

The Catechism of the Catholic Church explains: "Christ's Resurrection is the fulfillment of the promises both of the Old Testament and of Jesus himself during his earthly life. The phrase 'in accordance with the Scriptures' indicates that Christ's Resurrection fulfilled these predictions" (CCC 652).

He ascended into heaven, and is seated at the right hand of the Father

84. What do these words mean?

They refer to the mystery of Jesus' Ascension, which took place forty days after the Resurrection. Thus the Word, which had "come down from heaven," returned to heaven with the body He had assumed in the Incarnation.

85. Why did Jesus remain on earth forty days before ascending into Heaven?

Jesus remained on earth forty days before ascending into heaven to prove by various apparitions that He had truly risen, and to further instruct and confirm the Apostles in the truths of the faith.

During the forty days between His Resurrection and His Ascension, Jesus appeared many times to His Apostles to strengthen their faith

86. Why did Jesus ascend into heaven?

We must keep in mind that the term "heaven" means the Kingdom of God; therefore, Jesus ascended to take possession of the new kingdom, the kingdom of justice, love and peace, which began with His Passion, Death and Resurrection. From there He awaits us ("I go to prepare a place for you...that where I am, you also may be," Jn 14:2-3) and from there He sends His Holy Spirit for the sanctification of our souls.

87. What does it mean to say that Jesus is seated at the right hand of the Father?

This means that Jesus, as man, was the first to enter the glory of the Trinity, Father, Son and Holy Spirit, "so that at the name of Jesus every knee should bend of those in heaven, on earth and under the earth, and every tongue should confess that the Lord Jesus Christ is in the glory of the Father" (Phil 2:10-11).

He will come again in glory
to judge the living and the dead,
and His kingdom will have no end

Jesus will separate the just from the sinners as the shepherd divides the sheep from the goats. The just will be on His right and the sinners on His left

88. Will there be a second coming of Jesus?

Yes. His first coming took place in the hiddenness and humility of the Incarnation, when Jesus "appearing in the form of man ... humbled himself, becoming obedient to death, even to death on a cross" (Phil 2:7-8).

The second coming will take place at the end of time, when He will come in glory to judge the living and the dead.

89. How will the final judgment take place?

The final judgment is clearly described in the Gospel (Mt 25:31 ff): "But when the Son of Man shall come in his majesty, and all the angels with him, then he will sit on the throne of his glory; and before him will be gathered all the nations, and he will separate them one from another, as the shepherd separates the sheep from the goats; and he will set the sheep on his right hand, but the goats on the left. Then the king will say to those on his right hand, 'Come, blessed of my Father, take possession of the kingdom prepared for you from the foundation of the world.... Then he will say to those on his left hand, 'Depart from me, accursed ones, into the everlasting fire which was prepared for the devil and his angels.... And these will go into everlasting punishment, but the just into everlasting life."

90. At the final judgment will there be only two possibilities: eternal life or eternal damnation?

Yes.

"Then the king will say to those on his right hand, 'Come, blessed of
my Father, take possession of the kingdom prepared for you from the
foundation of the world.... Then he will say to those on his left hand, 'Depart
from me, accursed ones, into the everlasting fire which was prepared for the
devil and his angels.... And these will go into everlasting punishment, but
the just into everlasting life."

91. Will the soul only be judged at the final judgment, and not immediately after death?

No, there is also a judgment called the particular judgment which awaits us immediately after death. The

The particular judgment awaits us immediately after death

final judgment will only confirm the one which will already have been decided in this particular judgment. The difference between the two judgments is that, in the particular judgment, there is another possibility besides Heaven or Hell, that is, Purgatory. Purgatory is, however, only a temporary situation for those souls who are judged worthy of Paradise but who need some purification. Purgatory will come to an end for everyone at the final judgment.

"Each man receives his eternal retribution in his immortal soul at the very moment of his death, in a particular judgment that refers his life to Christ: either entrance into the blessedness of heaven—through a purification or immediately,—or immediate and everlasting damnation" (CCC 1022).

92. What will be the criteria for deciding whether a soul is worthy of Paradise, in need of Purgatory, or condemned to Hell?

If a person dies in the state of grace, that is, in God's friendship, his soul immediately goes either to Heaven or to Purgatory (if it is not perfectly purified). If, instead, the person dies in mortal sin, that is, outside the grace of God, he goes to Hell, far from God who is the source of all good, and he will remain there forever.

93. Why do we say that Jesus will come to judge the living and the dead?

We say this because Jesus will judge everyone without exception, even those who will still be alive on Judgment Day. Taken another way, this expression can indicate that Jesus will judge those who are spiritually alive through the life of grace, as well as those who are spiritually dead or lacking the life of grace.

94. Why do we say that Jesus' kingdom will have no end?

These words, which were spoken by the angel at the Annunciation (cf. Lk 1:33), signify that Jesus will forever be the glorious and immortal king of the whole universe. He is already reigning now, but His reign is not yet fully visible. It will become so when He returns in glory.

The angel Gabriel announced to the Virgin Mary
that Jesus' reign would have no end

I believe in the Holy Spirit, the Lord,
the giver of life, who proceeds
from the Father and the Son.
who with the Father and Son is
adored and glorified, who has
spoken through the prophets

95. The Creed contains a great variety of names for the Holy Spirit as well as for the Word. Why?

This is because, just as in regard to the Word, the Creed was composed in response to the Arian heresy, so in regard to the Holy Spirit, the Creed is a response to those who denied His divinity. In addition to the names contained in the Creed, the Catechism of the Catholic Church (692-693) mentions many others, all taken from Sacred Scripture. Among these are the names *Paraclete, Consoler, Spirit of Truth, Spirit of Christ,* and *Spirit of God.*

96. So the Holy Spirit is just as much God as the Father and the Son?

Yes, beyond the slightest doubt. This is our faith. All the expressions found in the Creed ("Lord and giver of life"..."who has spoken through the Prophets") can only refer to God.

In the Creed we say that the Holy Spirit has spoken through the Prophets

97. Why do we say that the Holy Spirit proceeds from the Father and the Son?

We say this because the Father does not spirate (breathe forth) the Holy Spirit by Himself, but does so together with the Son. Therefore we must say that the Son proceeds from the Father alone by way of generation, but the Holy Spirit proceeds from the Father and the Son as from an only source by way of spiration (breathing forth).

98. How can we understand the spiration of the Holy Spirit?

This is a great mystery. But even here Western theology, thanks above all to St. Augustine and St. Thomas Aquinas (as already seen in the case of the generation of the Word), has attempted to find an explanation of the spiration of the Holy Spirit. Just as the Word proceeds from the Father by way of knowledge, so the Holy Spirit proceeds from the Father and the Son as from one principle, by way of love. The Holy Spirit, according to this interpretation, is therefore the love between the Father and the Son, or better, He is the Person who proceeds from the love between the Father and the Son. Thus we can say that the life of the Trinity concludes in love, and we understand better the marvelous expression of the Apostle St. John (1 Jn 4:8): "God is love." This love, God has "poured forth in our hearts by the Holy Spirit who has been given to us" (Rm 5:5).

99. We say that the Son was sent at the moment of the Incarnation (Gal 4:4). Can we also say that the Holy Spirit has been sent?

Yes, we can say this. Even though it is true that the Holy Spirit has always been at work in human history (for example, speaking through the prophets), and above

all by acting in the depths of souls for their sanctification, we must, however, hold that He was visibly sent on Pentecost, and that on that day He took definitive possession of the Church, which on that day started her great mission of salvation in human history.

The Holy Spirit is the love between the Father and the Son. St. John says that "God is love"

I believe in one, holy, catholic and apostolic Church

Even if a church is small and plain, it is always the image of the entire Church as a "community of believers"

100. What is the Church?

The Church is a very rich and complex reality which can be defined and described in various ways. She is the community of believers in Jesus Christ, so united in Him as to be defined as His body. The Church's life comes from the Holy Spirit, who is the principle of her unity and life.

Vatican Council II, in the dogmatic constitution *Lumen Gentium,* describes the Church under various aspects, principally these:
- The Church is the *Kingdom of Christ,* already mysteriously present (n. 3);
- The Church is the *seed and the beginning* of the kingdom of God (n. 5);
- The Church is the *Body of Christ* and *His Spouse* (n. 7);

• The Church is the *Temple of the Holy Spirit* (n. 4);
• The Church is the *New People of God*, which prolongs and completes the mystery of the elect of the Old Testament (n. 9). The Church finds her most perfect fulfillment, image and model in the Blessed Virgin Mary (nos. 63-65).

The Church is guided by the bishops headed by the Pope, the successor of St. Peter

101. Is the Church only an invisible community?

No, the Church is also visible and has a very precise structure. She is guided by the Bishops, who are the successors of the Apostles, with the Pope at their head. The Pope is the successor of St. Peter.

102. What does it mean to say that the Church is one?

To say that the Church is one means that she is undivided. She professes only one faith; she is one in her common acts of worship; she has only one Eucharist which both represents and brings about unity. She has one *visible* head, the Pope, while her *invisible* principle of unity is also one: the Holy Spirit.

103. But if the Church is one and undivided, why are there divisions among Christians?

There are divisions because Christians are weak and imperfect. Thus, over the course of centuries, some communities separated themselves from the unity of the Church. Therefore they are not perfectly incorporated into the one Church founded by Jesus, the Catholic Church, even though they conserve—some more and some less—many elements of holiness and truth. For example, they might conserve, as a minimum, the acceptance of Holy Scripture as the Word of God, and Baptism in the name of the Father and of the Son and of the Holy Spirit.

104. Why do we say that the Church is holy?

The Pope, head of the Church, makes use of the particular assistance of the Holy Spirit

We say that the Church is holy because her Founder, Jesus, is holy; her life principle, the Holy Spirit, is holy; her teachings are holy and sanctifying; her sacraments are holy and sanctifying; and finally, her life, which is none other than the life of grace, is holy.

105. So are all the Church's members holy?

"[The Church] is therefore holy, though she has sinners in her bosom, because she herself has no other life but that of grace: it is by living by her life that her members are sanctified; it is by removing themselves from her life that they fall into sins and disorders that prevent the radiation of her sanctity. This is why she suffers and does penance for these offenses, of which she has the power to heal her children through the blood of Christ and the gift of the Holy Spirit" (Paul VI, *Credo of the People of God,* 19).

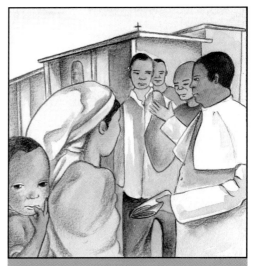

The Church is catholic because she possesses the fullness of the means of salvation and because she was sent to the entire human race

106. Why do we say that the Church is catholic?

The word *catholic* signifies *universal,* whether in regard to totality or in regard to integrality. Now the Church is said to be catholic in two senses. "First, the Church is catholic because Christ is present in her. 'Where there is Christ Jesus, there is the Catholic Church.' In her subsists the fullness of Christ's body united with its head; this implies that she receives from him 'the fullness of the means of salvation' which he has willed: correct and complete confession of faith, full sacramental life, and ordained ministry in apostolic succession" (CCC 830).

The Church is also catholic because she was sent on a mission by Christ to the entire human race. In this second sense she is catholic because she is scattered

The Church is linked uninterruptedly to the Apostles; the Bishops, in fact, are their successors

throughout the whole world and is always expanding. She is catholic because she embraces all times and cultures. She is catholic because her teaching is directed to all men and women. She is catholic also because she embraces not only the men and women of this earth, but also the angels, the souls of the blessed in Paradise, and the souls in Purgatory.

107. Why do we say that the Church is apostolic?

We say this because the Church can be traced back without interruption to the Apostles (apostolicity of her origin); because her teaching is what the Apostles transmitted (apostolicity of doctrine); and because she is governed by Bishops, who are successors of the Apostles, traceable back to them through an uninterrupted line of episcopal ordination, by which every Bishop can be traced back through time to one of the Apostles (apostolicity of succession).

I confess one Baptism for the forgiveness of sins

108. What is the relationship between Baptism and the forgiveness of sin?

"Our Lord tied the forgiveness of sins to faith and Baptism: 'Go into all the world and preach the gospel to the whole creation. He who believes and is baptized will be saved' (Mk 16:15-16). Baptism is the first and chief sacrament of forgiveness of sins because it unites us with Christ" (CCC 977).

Baptism is the first sacrament for the forgiveness of sin because it unites us with God

109. What does the "forgiveness of sin" mean?

Baptism is like a ray of light which dispels the darkness of original sin

Sin means distancing ourselves from God. The "forgiveness of sin" means the pardon of sin, and consequently drawing closer to God, who calls us to become His friends, as Jesus said: "I no longer call you servants, but friends." Baptism, therefore, wipes out sin and gives us friendship with God, which we usually call "grace."

110. Can only Baptism remit sin?

Baptism remits sin but does not free our nature from its weakness; thus we often fall back into sin. So it was necessary for the Church, the community of believers in Jesus Christ, to have an additional way to remit sin besides the Sacrament of Baptism, which we receive only once. For this reason Jesus Christ instituted the Sacrament of Penance, or confession, by which the Church, through the Bishops and priests, can forgive any repentant sinner for any sin committed after Baptism until the day of death.

111. Why do we say "one Baptism"?

Baptism unites us to Christ, in particular to His Passion, Death and Resurrection, and makes us Christians. In every Baptism, then, it is Christ who baptizes, incorporating the one baptized into Himself or uniting the person to Himself. Now there is only one way to be united to Christ, and this is by Baptism when it is celebrated validly, that is, when the person baptized believes that Christ is the Son of God made man and the only Savior.

112. Is Baptism of water the only means for receiving the forgiveness of sin?

Ordinarily, yes; for those who are not already baptized, Baptism of water is the only means. We must keep in mind, however, that the Church has always recognized three forms of Baptism: Baptism of water (sacramental Baptism), Baptism of blood, and Baptism of desire. Baptism of blood is martyrdom undergone in order to remain faithful to the Christian faith. Baptism of desire takes place when an unbaptized person, under the influence of grace, repents of his sins for the love of God (that is, he makes an act of perfect contrition) and desires Baptism, even if only implicitly. Through this last kind of Baptism (Baptism of desire), the possibility of salvation is open even to those who do not explicitly know Jesus Christ and His Church.

Baptism of blood is martyrdom suffered in order to remain faithful to God

I look forward to the resurrection of the dead and the life of the world to come. Amen.

113. What does "the resurrection of the dead" mean?

At the moment of death the soul is separated from the body, to which it will be reunited later in the "resurrection of the dead"

"The resurrection of the dead" means that every soul separated from the body will be reunited to the body he had in this life. Belief in the resurrection of the dead is an essential element of the Christian faith: "...just as Christ is truly risen from the dead and lives for ever, so after death the righteous will live for ever with the risen Christ and he will raise them up on the last day" (CCC 989).

114. When will the resurrection take place?

The resurrection of the dead will take place at the end of the world, when Jesus will return in glory to judge the living and the dead.

115. Will all men and women rise again in the same condition?

No, there will be a tremendous difference between the bodies of the blessed and the bodies of the damned, because only the bodies of the elect will resemble Jesus' glorious body.

116. What does "the life of the world to come" mean?

It means that life which men and women will have for all eternity in the "new heavens and the new earth," as St. Peter says (2 Pt 3:13), the life that will take place after our time in the world in which we now live. At present we cannot imagine the details of this "world to come." We know with certainty, however, that the conditions of the blessed and of the damned will be different. The blessed will be in full and definitive happiness, because they will enjoy God, the Supreme Good; the damned, instead, will find themselves in a state of suffering without end, because they will never enter the presence of God.

117. In what will the happiness of the blessed consist?

The happiness of the blessed will consist in the vision of God, the Supreme Good; love will follow upon the vision, and complete and perfect happiness will follow upon love. To this will be added the joy of the company of Jesus, Mary, the angels and saints, and the enjoyment of all the beauties of the new world. Every human desire will be fully fulfilled in a complete and definitive way: "And [the servants of God] shall see his face and his name shall be on their foreheads. And night shall be no more, and they shall have no need of light of lamp, or light of sun, for the Lord God will shed light upon them; and they shall reign forever and ever" (Rv 22:4-5).

118. In what will the suffering of the damned consist?

The suffering of the damned will consist above all in the privation of the vision of God Who is the Source of all good. This privation will give rise to suffering so intense that at present we cannot even begin to imagine it.

In Paradise the blessed, along with all the angels and saints, will see the glory of God

119. Will the joys of Paradise and the sufferings of Hell be equal for all?

No, the measure of joy for each of the blessed will depend on each one's level of holiness, though each will possess the fullness of joy in a completely fulfilling way.

On the other hand, the level of suffering of the damned will depend on how much sin is in their hearts—sin which in life brought them to obstinately oppose God and His commandments, and which continues to remain in their will, which is definitively fixed against God.

120. What does the word "Amen" at the end of the Creed mean?

This word means "So be it" or, "I believe with absolute certainty that everything contained in the Creed or Symbol which I have just recited is absolutely true, because God revealed it and the Church infallibly teaches it, so I can accept it with a firm faith."

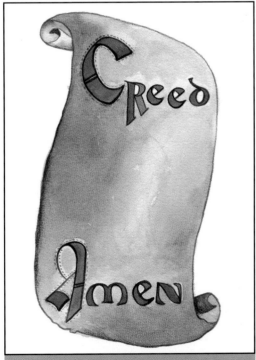

The word *Amen* at the end of the Creed means "So be it," that is, "I hold as true all that is affirmed in the Symbol".

121. How can we make these truths of the faith our own and strengthen our Christian life so that we may share it with others?

It is vitally necessary that we become persons of habitual prayer. The Christian life cannot be lived without prayer, that is, without constant contact with God. St. Paul tells us in 1 Thess 5:17: "Pray constantly." In prayer we can come to understand these truths more deeply and live them more fully. Thus we will be more courageous in using the graces of Confirmation to bring Christ to others.

PART III

WITNESSES FOR THE FAITH

All Christians who live their faith authentically become witnesses for the faith. Among them, however, there are many particularly radiant examples who have become models for the People of God. These are, in a special way, the martyrs and the saints.

Jesus' gaze transformed each person into a child of God. God's children always desire to witness to the love of their Heavenly Father

A. Martyrs

The most glorious pages of the Church's history are those written in the blood of her martyrs. The 20th century, more than any other period in her history, can be described as the century of martyrs, so great was the number of Christians who witnessed to their faith by giving their lives.

But who are the martyrs? The term *martyr* comes from the Greek and means *witness.* Already in the New Testament, particularly in the case of St. Stephen in the Acts of the Apostles, we see the figure of one who offers his life as witness to his own love for Christ. Martyrdom is a real participation in the Passion and Death of Jesus on the Cross, because Christ is our model and He witnessed to the point of giving His own life.

Martyrdom is a bloody testimony, but it strengthens the Church's faith and makes her more mission-minded and more desirous of spreading the Kingdom of God throughout the whole world.

The Martyrs of the First Three Centuries

During Nero's persecution, St. Peter was crucified and St. Paul was beheaded

As we have already seen, the first martyr was St. Stephen, but he was soon followed by all the Apostles except St. John, who still had to undergo harsh trials. In a very particular way the Church celebrates the martyrdom at Rome of the two great Apostles, Peter and Paul. St. Clement tells us of the first terrible persecution, which lasted four years (from 64-68 AD) under Nero. It was unleashed by the false accusation that the Christians had been the cause of the terrible fire that destroyed the entire city of Rome in 10 days.

Many Christians were given as food to the lions

In the year 112, the great Roman historian Tacitus, in his *Annals,* wrote: "Nero, in order to stamp out public accusations that he himself had started the fire, accused those among the people who are called Christians of being the true culprits, and he subjected them to the most cruel tortures and death."

These first martyrs refused to renounce their faith in Christ even to save their lives, and for this they were put to death in the most horrible ways. Some were thrown to the lions in the circus; others were crucified and then set on fire as human torches in the night.

The persecutions against the Christians lasted for three more centuries, and the most terrible among them were those of Decian in 250 AD and Diocletian in 303 AD.

Finally, in the year 313, the Emperor Constantine promulgated an edict which solemnly recognized Christians' full right to profess and follow their own Faith and allowed monastic life, the free exercise of religion, and the building of new churches.

St. Clement I, Pope and Martyr

Other Martyrs of the First Millennium

Once these persecutions came to an end, however, the testimony of martyrdom within the Church continued. For example, in 5th century Africa, thousands of Catholics were martyred during the persecution by the Vandals. Later, in the 7th and 8th centuries, during the Muslims' rapid conquest of North Africa and Spain, many Christians were slain for refusing to renounce their Catholic faith.

Among others we remember the eight hundred martyrs of Otranto (some centuries later) who, upon refusing to convert to Islam, were all beheaded.

The Martyrs of the Second Millennium

Among the most painful persecutions for the Church were those which broke out within Christianity itself following schisms and heresies. In 1534, Henry VIII, king of England, proclaimed himself head of the Church in that country. He not only took possession of all the Catholic Church's goods and property, but also demanded full and complete submission from everyone—subjects, priests and religious. Many faithful Catholics, religious and bishops, refused to obey his unjust commands. Among them we especially remember St. Thomas More, a friend and influential counselor to the king, who chose, at the cost of his life, to remain faithful to the Pope rather than give in to the threats and the bribes offered him. His example would later be imitated by thousands of the faithful in Great Britain.

At Gorkum, Holland, in 1572, St. Nicholas Pick and 18 of his companions were arrested and put to death by the Calvinists for defending the authority of the Roman Church and the Real Presence of Christ in the Eucharist. Holland, in fact, after having become mostly Calvinist—in order to obtain political independence from Spain, among other reasons—began a ruthless repression of anything that reminded people of the Catholic faith.

Many martyrs were subjected to horrible tortures before they died. This happened especially in countries where

Christian culture had not yet had an influence, as in Canada on the part of the Iroquois, and in the Far East (China, Japan, Korea, Vietnam, etc.) on the part of the local authorities. These martyrs wrote perhaps the most beautiful pages in all the Church's history. We cannot forget them.

In countries which had long been influenced by Christianity, we remember the martyrs of the French Revolution, particularly the Catholics of the Vendee, who were exterminated *en masse* because they wanted to remain totally faithful to the Church and to the Pope. In effect, the result was the genocide of the Vendean people; it often happened that because "holy mother guillotine was too slow" and "shooting took too long and used too much gunpowder and too many bullets," people were boarded in groups of a hundred at a time onto large rafts, which were floated out to the middle of the river and then sunk.

Notwithstanding all this, contrary to what might appear to be true, it was the 1900s—a century of formidable scientific progress and the century which saw the Universal Charter of the Rights of Man—which saw the greatest persecution ever of the world's Christians. It is impossible to count the number of martyrs. The estimates, (which can only be approximate), gleaned from formerly secret archives, seem to indicate that many more than 50 million persons were killed (many more were persecuted and had their religious liberty curtailed).

Particularly cruel were the persecutions in Mexico during the first decades of the 20th century, and those in Spain in the 1930s. The former were organized by the anticlericals and the latter by the Communists. In Spain more than 6,800 priests and religious were massacred, not counting the more numerous lay people who were martyred.

Then there were the victims of Nazism and the much more numerous victims of Soviet Communism.

The relentless war against Christians which marked the two great totalitarian regimes of the century—Communism and Nazism—has been taken up today with renewed vigor by

In the 20th century more than 50 million people were martyred for their faith

fundamentalist Islam. Sudan, Nigeria, Pakistan, Indonesia, and Saudi Arabia are a few among the countries where freely professing the Christian creed means risking one's life.

In a particular way, in Sudan from the 1980s until today, more than two million Christians have been killed, while those who remain suffer displacement, the plundering of their harvests and the systematic destruction of their crops. The children who have been orphaned or have been stolen by slave traffickers, are forced to convert to Islam or else be sold as slaves.

The Church of the first millennium was born of the blood of the martyrs, as Tertullian said: "The blood of martyrs is the seed of Christians." Today the Church has become once again the Church of the martyrs. The persecutions of believers—priests, religious and laity—have sown a great seed of martyrs in all parts of the world. Their witness and their charity strengthen our faith.

B. The Saints

The Christian saints are people who lived their faith in a consistent way, reaching the level of heroism in the practice of virtue. The saints, known and unknown, are countless. Here we will recount the stories of only a few particularly significant saints.

St. Anthony the Abbot (251-356)
Father of Eastern Monasticism

The devil tried to frighten St. Anthony

Many of the stories about Anthony's life come down to us from the writings of the bishop St. Athanasius (a Doctor of the Church), who met Anthony a year before the latter's death. Anthony was born around the year 251 in Coma, Egypt. He was about 20 when his parents, who owned a large amount of land, died, leaving him alone with his sister. One day, when he was in church, Anthony was deeply struck by the Gospel passage in which Jesus said to the rich young man: "If you wish to be perfect, go, sell what you have, give to the poor and you will

In the desert, St. Anthony the Abbot tamed the most ferocious lions by showing them the crucifix

have treasure in heaven; then come, follow me." Anthony decided to give away all his goods to the people of his village, keeping only enough to support his sister, whom he entrusted to some religious women. Then he dedicated himself to the ascetical life in solitude, subjecting himself to severe discipline. He worked with his own hands to earn his living, and part of what he earned he gave away as alms.

Everyone loved Anthony; the people called him "the friend of God." But, as St. Athanasius relates, "the devil, who hates anything good and is full of envy, could not bear to see a young person leading such a holy life, and began to stir up trouble for him." The devil first tried to get St. Anthony to give up his ascetical practices and prayers, reminding him of his riches, his affection for his relatives, his desire for glory, and the pleasures of rich foods; he often took on the form of a beautiful woman in order to seduce him. But Anthony, keeping his thoughts fixed on Christ and meditating on the value of the soul, conquered these temptations. In fact, he said that "the heart gains strength as the pleasures of the body weaken."

The devil tried to keep St. Anthony from going to Alexandria in Egypt by showing him a heap of gold coins

During his long life of 105 years, Anthony worked many miracles. The Lord also granted him the gift of being able to comfort others, and thus Anthony "consoled the afflicted, reconciled those in conflict and repeated to all that nothing in the world must be preferred to the love of Christ. He convinced many to embrace the solitary life, and thus the desert became a city of monks.... Often Anthony exhorted his brothers to stand firm against the devil's wiles, warning them that the demons pretend to predict the future, interpret Sacred Scripture, or to be angels."

During Maximus' persecution of the Church, Anthony went to Alexandria to console the persecuted Christians there. Once the persecution was over, he retired again to his solitary dwelling. But since his recollection was frequently disturbed by the growing crowds who came to see him, he decided to retire to the top of a very high mountain. Here, too, he suffered many attacks from the demons.

Before he died, he called some of the monks and said to them, "I am going the way of the Fathers. I see that the Lord is calling me. Be vigilant and live as if you were to die each day."

On January 17, 356, Anthony died, leaving as his legacy a way which countless generations of monks of both East and West have since followed.

St. Benedict the Abbot (480-547)
Founder of the Benedictine Order; Co-patron of Europe

St. Benedict in prayer before the crucifix

St. Benedict was born in the little town of Norcia, Italy, around the year 480 AD, in a particularly dramatic historical period. Four years earlier, with the overthrow of the last emperor, Romulus Augustus, the Western Roman Empire had crumbled. Benedict's well-to-do family sent him to study in Rome, and in that city the young Benedict, fascinated by the example of St. Anthony the Abbot, decided to give up his studies, his home, and his inheritance in order to live in solitude and poverty. He retired to a place called Subiaco, where he met a hermit by the name of Romanus who offered to help him. Romanus divested Benedict of his rich

St. Benedict saved a drowning boy

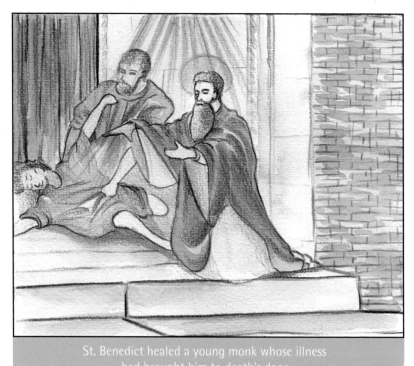

St. Benedict healed a young monk whose illness
had brought him to death's door

clothing and covered him with a simple goatskin garment as
a sign of his consecration to God.

Benedict spent three years in extreme poverty, in medi-
tation and profound prayer, fighting temptations to return to
his former life. However, he came through all this successfully
with God's help, which he implored with unceasing prayer.

Though he lived a solitary life, the fame of his holiness spread rapidly. Upon the death of the superior of a small
religious community, the monks came to beg him to become
their superior. The holy man firmly refused for a long time.
His main reason was his conviction that the harshness of his
rule could not be reconciled with the monks' practical way of
life. But in the end, since they insisted, he agreed and came
to live in the monastery.

As superior Benedict carefully watched over the small
community. He was inflexible in correcting, yet quick to forgive others' errors.

His rigorous methods quickly gave rise to discontent and opposition in some of the brothers, who decided to murder him. At table one day, according to their usual custom, they presented the superior with a cup of wine—only this time it had been poisoned. However, as soon as Benedict traced the sign of the cross over it, the cup shattered. Death gave way as a result of the life-giving blessing in Christ's name.

Benedict formulated a new rule which ever afterwards formed Benedictine monastic life: *Ora et labora* (pray and work). This would become an anchor for many—for the young Romans, both nobles and common citizens, fleeing the moral and civil unrest of the cities, and for the young barbarians who wished to live their new-found faith in Christ in community. In this way St. Benedict laid the foundations for a new kind of community life uniting the Latin and barbarian peoples—a foundation based on Christ and His Church.

St. Benedict, tracing the sign of the cross,
shattered the cup of poisoned wine
which some hostile monks had offered him

St. Dominic venerating the crucifix

St. Dominic Guzman (1170-1221)
Founder of the Order of Preachers (Dominicans)

Dominic was born at Caleruega, Spain, around the year 1170. As a boy, he was entrusted to the care of his uncle, an archpriest, to be educated in the truths of the faith and to receive elementary instruction. Sent to Valencia to pursue his studies, he worked with diligence and love.

When a famine struck the city, he sold his books and everything else he owned in order to give something to the poor. To those who were astonished at his depriving himself of the means to study, he responded with these few words, the first of his words which have come down to us: "I do not want to study from lifeless parchments while people are dying of hunger." The example of his charity touched the hearts of professors and theologians, who began to be more generous to the poor.

Dominic prayed and studied day and night and continually begged God to let him dedicate himself completely to the salvation of souls. When Diego, elected bishop of Osma in 1201, had to go on a delicate diplomatic mission to Denmark, he chose Dominic, who by now was a priest, to accompany him.

In 1206, on the way back from a second trip to Denmark, Diego and Dominic stopped in Rome to ask the Pope's

St. Dominic calmed the raging waters of a river and saved a group of pilgrims with a sign of the cross

permission to dedicate themselves to the evangelization of the pagans of the North. But Innocent III sent them to preach against the Albigensian heretics in Southern France. They obeyed and left for that land.

Bishop Diego, however, died suddenly on December 30, 1207, leaving Dominic alone to preach against the heretics. Dominic took part in many public debates, personal conversations, negotiations, and preaching, meanwhile offering prayers and penances.

In 1215, when Foulques, the Bishop of Toulouse, decided to name him diocesan preacher, it was the beginning of a new mission for Dominic. He gathered many companions around himself, giving his preaching a stable and organized form. Then, together with Foulques, he went back to the Pope to present his great plan for preaching to the heretics.

The following year, on December 22, Pope Honorius III gave his official approval to the "Holy Preaching" of Toulouse.

In the summer of 1217, the holy founder sent his spiritual sons into Europe, mostly to Paris and Bologna, where there were prestigious universities. In 1220 and 1221, Dominic presided over two general chapters whose purpose was to rewrite their *Magna Charta* and to specify the foundational elements of the Order: preaching, study, mendicant poverty, communal

St. Dominic challenged the Catharist heretics by his preaching in Southern France: the heretics' book burned, while the Gospel was miraculously unharmed

life, legislation, geographic distribution, and missionary activity.

Worn out by his apostolic labors, Dominic died on August 6, 1221, surrounded by his brothers at his beloved convent in Bologna. Gregory XI canonized him on July 3, 1234.

The spiritual image of St. Dominic is unmistakable: he himself, during the difficult years of apostolate against the Albigensian heresy, defined himself as a "humble preaching servant." The foundation of his life is a precise apostolic program: to lovingly witness to Christ before others by giving them the Truth in evangelical poverty. All the witnesses of St. Dominic's life revealed the twofold orientation of his activity: always attuned to interior and divine realities, always open to one's neighbor.

St. Francis of Assisi
(1181-1226) Founder of the Order of Friars Minor

St. Francis loved all creatures
and considered them
brothers and sisters in the Lord

The earliest information we have on St. Francis' young life is found in the *Fonti Francescane:* "There lived in Assisi a man by the name of Francis, who from his earliest years was educated by his parents according to the vanities of the world."

At twenty, Francis fought in the war between Assisi and Perugia. He was captured and thrown into prison, where he remained for almost a year. During that time he became gravely ill and nearly died. This gave rise to the difficult path of his conversion.

One day, while walking down the street, he came upon a leper who was begging. Francis stopped and looked at the sick man's wounds with horror. He wanted to run away from this man whose flesh was rotting, but suddenly he remembered a promise he had made to the Lord while he was in prison: to become a knight of Christ if he ever got out alive. He got off his horse and gave the poor man some money. Immediately the thought of Christ's Passion, of Jesus nailed to the Cross, came to his mind; moved to tears, he recognized the Lord in that leper, and embraced him.

A difficult period now began for Francis: he visited the lepers, gave away his possessions to the beggars he met, and retired to pray in isolated places.

The Pope had a vision of St. Francis holding up the crumbling Basilica of St. Peter

One day he entered the nearly-ruined Church of San Damiano and knelt before the crucifix, imploring a sign showing him what he should do. In the silence of the shadows he heard a loud voice which said three times, "Francis, go and repair my house, which, as you see, is in ruins." The saint did not immediately understand the real meaning of the message; he thought he was to physically repair the little church. In order to do this he sold more of his possessions to pay the workers.

This episode angered Francis' father, who, exasperated, publicly disowned him, had him banished from the city, and dragged him before the Bishop, thinking that the latter, by his religious authority, could force his son to obey him. Francis passed between two rows of silent and curious people. He stripped himself and handed his clothes to his father, saying, "Up till now I called you my father on earth, but from now on I can say with all certainty: Our Father who art in heaven, be-

Baby Jesus appeared to St. Francis

cause I have placed all my store in Him; in Him have I placed all my trust and hope." The Bishop, moved by such a witness of faith, covered him with his cloak and embraced him, giving him his blessing.

From that moment on Francis lived in the greatest poverty, and many followed him along this way.

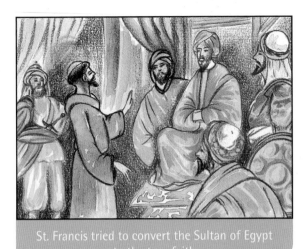

St. Francis tried to convert the Sultan of Egypt to the true faith

Thus the Franciscan Order was born, one of the most important and well-known orders in the Church.

Our saint was always particularly devoted to the Passion of Christ, and he received the stigmata, a sign of his perfect imitation of the poor, crucified Jesus.

St. Francis died in Assisi on October 3, 1226, and was canonized less than two years later on July 15, 1228.

Two years before his death, St. Francis received the stigmata on Mt. Verna

During his life, St. Ignatius had many visions which strengthened his faith and his decision to dedicate himself completely to God

St. Ignatius of Loyola
(1491-1556)
Founder of the Society of Jesus

St. Ignatius was born in 1491 in Loyola, in the Basque region of Spain, of a family of lesser nobility. As a young man he frequented the royal court and participated in the war between Spain and France. Wounded in the siege of Pamplona in 1521, he was carried back to the family castle of Loyola.

During his recovery he was given the *Life of Christ* and the lives of some saints to read. Ignatius was profoundly touched by these writings. Up till that moment his interests had been concentrated on military affairs and worldly things, but reading the lives of Jesus and the saints made him want to imitate them more and more.

One night, while he was still awake, he had a vision of Our Lady with the Child Jesus. He contemplated this scene at length, and, fascinated by Mary's maternal love and by the fraternal affection of Jesus, he received the greatest consolation. He made a decision to radically change his lifestyle: now he thought only about becoming a true "soldier of Christ."

As soon as he was healed he traveled to Montserrat, in Catalonia, to the Shrine of the Black Madonna. There he exchanged his sword and dagger for a pilgrim's staff. He made a long, detailed general confession of his whole sinful life to

St. Ignatius teaching children the catechism

the Benedictine master of novices. On the eve of the feast of the Annunciation in 1522, he met a poor man with whom he exchanged garments. Then he went to the city of Manresa where he remained for about a year, having many extraordinary mystical experiences.

A little while later he decided to make a pilgrimage to the Holy Land with the intention of remaining there, but he encountered many difficulties. In the end he returned to Spain where he dedicated himself to the spiritual care of some friends, making use of the book he had written, the famous *Spiritual Exercises,* in which he had recorded all his interior experiences with the aim of helping others to conquer their own disordered passions.

Later, in Paris, he met Francis Xavier and Peter Favre, who would become his first companions and with whom, together with four other friends, he would officially begin the Society of Jesus.

In 1540 Ignatius sent Francis Xavier to the missions in India. The Rule of the Society of Jesus was

On August 15, 1534, in the Church of St. Mary at Montmartre, St. Ignatius, along with some companions, began the Society of Jesus, which was approved by Pope Paul III in 1540

definitively approved by Paul III on September 27, 1540. Ignatius, elected the first Superior General for life, immediately dedicated himself to writing the first Constitutions for the new Order, whose motto became: *Ad majorem Dei gloriam* (For the greater glory of God), and to greater care of souls. While he wrote the Constitutions he had many visions which confirmed some of the points he was writing. Sometimes he saw God the Father, other times the three Persons of the Trinity, or the Blessed Mother interceding or approving, or Jesus, who often appeared to him as radiant as the sun.

Ad maiorem Dei gloriam—"For the greater glory of God"—is the motto of the Jesuits (the Society of Jesus) founded by St. Ignatius

Ignatius died in Rome on July 31, 1556, and was canonized in 1622.

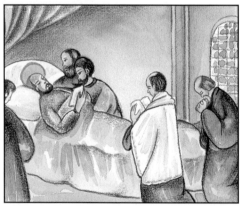

St. Ignatius died in Rome on July 31, 1556, and was canonized on March 12, 1622

St. Francis Xavier (1506-1552)
Patron of the Missions

St. Francis Xavier is one of the most important Jesuit saints. In fact, besides being one of St. Ignatius of Loyola's first companions and thus one of the first Jesuits in history, he is also considered the missionary saint *par excellence*. This pioneer of the missions of modern times, declared patron of the East in 1748, of the Society for the Propagation of the Faith in 1904, and of all the missions, together with St. Therese of the Child Jesus, in 1927, was born in 1506 of noble parents in the Xavier family castle in Navarre, Spain. At nineteen he went to study at the Sorbonne in Paris. He was given a room at the College of St. Barbara, where St. Ignatius and Bl. Peter Favre were also students.

His encounter with Ignatius—who immediately saw Francis' greatness of soul, in spite of his worldly ambitions—was decisive. "Such a great heart and noble soul," said Ignatius to Francis one day, "can never be content with ephemeral worldly loves. Your ambition must be for the glory that lasts for all eternity." On August 15, 1534, Francis joined Ignatius and five others in consecrating himself to God for life in the church of Montmartre in Paris.

While he was still in Paris, Francis was named papal legate, and on April 7, 1541, he set sail in a ship bound directly for India. In those days such a long sea voyage meant danger and sickness, hunger and thirst, terrible cold and heat, storms and sudden calms which could immobilize the ship for long periods of time.

After years of intense missionary activity in India, Francis reached Japan where he converted many by his preaching and example. He made many contacts with the Buddhist monks, debated with the bonzes (who later tried to hinder him) and other dignitaries, and was finally received by the emperor.

One of his traveling companions wrote of what they had to suffer together: intense cold and snowstorms; pirates at sea and bandits on land; nights spent in the open because there were no inns; scorn from those they met, since they were poorly dressed and malnourished; frequent hunger and thirst.

Francis noted with satisfaction that the Church in Japan was already growing, so he decided to go back to the first communities he had founded. After a dangerous and difficult journey, he reached Mallorca, where to his immense joy he found several letters which had reached him from Europe. In one of these letters, written by Fr. Ignatius of Loyola, he read that he had been appointed Superior of the Society of Jesus in the new Province of India.

St. Francis Xavier, after having preached with abundant results in Goa and in the Mallorcas, went to Japan where he stayed four years

He took up his travels once more and reached Goa in early February.

Francis had always dreamed of going to China so that he could carry the light of the Gospel into that land as well. He managed to make the journey, but as soon as he set foot in China, he fell gravely ill. At dawn on December 3, 1552, at the age of 46, he died with the name of Jesus on his lips.

Even though Francis was never able to start a real and continuous work of Christianization in China, he can be

considered the first missionary to that country, which was certainly made fruitful by his great desire to evangelize it.

It is estimated that, thanks to the ardent zeal of this great missionary saint, about 30,000 persons were baptized. Gregory XV canonized him on March 12, 1622.

St. Francis Xavier always had a burning desire to bring the Word of God to China. But when he reached the Chinese coast, worn out by his labors and by the cold, he died on December 3, 1552

St. Maria Goretti (1890-1902)
Virgin and Martyr

St. Maria Goretti was born in Corinaldo, Italy, on October 16, 1890, to a family of poor farmers. In 1899, hoping for a better future, her parents moved to Ferriere di Conca, a marshy area. Shortly afterward, however, Maria's father died of malaria at the age of only 41.

In this painful situation Maria refused to be discouraged and said to her mother, Assunta,

Shortly before dying, St. Maria Goretti saw a beautiful Lady "surrounded by light and flowers": the Blessed Virgin Mary

"Mamma, don't worry. I'll take care of the housework and you take Papa's place in the fields. God will not abandon us!" At the young age of ten little Maria already had great determination and an unshakable faith, taking upon herself the responsibility of caring for her little brothers and sisters.

To go to school would never be anything more than a dream for her. At the cost of great sacrifice she was able to attend catechism classes and make her First Communion on the feast of Corpus Christi. That day, Maria asked two things of Jesus: Heaven for her father, and, for herself, the grace to become holier each day.

Unfortunately, Alessandro, an 18-year-old boy, had lustful thoughts toward Maria and began to torment her with impure suggestions and even death threats if she did not comply. On Saturday, July 5, 1902, Alessandro, blinded by passion, found some trivial excuse to leave his work in the fields and went to the house where Maria was. During the process for her beatification he himself described that day:

"I grabbed her roughly by the arm and, since she resisted, I dragged her into the kitchen and kicked the door closed. She understood immediately that I was going to make the same attempt I had made twice before, and she said to me, 'No, no, God does not want this! If you do this you'll go to Hell!' Seeing that she absolutely refused to go along with my filthy intentions, I was overcome with fury and, taking the knife, began to stab her in the stomach...."

The poor girl lived 24 hours in terrible pain. She was delirious and imagined herself still under the knife's blows. She cried out, "What are you doing, Alessandro? You'll go to Hell. It's a sin, it's a sin!" Suddenly she exclaimed, "What a beautiful lady!" Noticing the incredulity of those around her, she added, "Can't you see her? Look, she's so beautiful, surrounded by light and flowers." It was 3:45 PM on July 6, 1902. Her Calvary was finished.

Alessandro Serenelli was condemned to thirty years in prison. During the first years he gave no sign of repentance. But one night, as he recounted, he dreamed that Maria told him that he, too, could reach Paradise, and from that moment onward he changed his life. He grew close to God and offered his sufferings in reparation for his sins. He was released 27 years after his crime, and his first act was to go to the Saint's mother and ask her forgiveness.

On June 24, 1950, in the presence of her mother and of Alessandro, Pope Pius XII canonized Maria Goretti.

Blessed Mother Teresa of Calcutta (1910-1997)
Foundress of the Missionaries of Charity

Blessed Mother Teresa of Calcutta always cared for the humblest, the most defenseless, the children, the abandoned old people and the poorest of the poor

Gonxha Agnes Bojaxhiu, the future Mother Teresa, was born August 26, 1910 in Skopje, Yugoslavia. Her family, whose ancestry was Albanian, was deeply Catholic. At age 18 Gonxha felt called to the religious life. She was received into the Sisters of Our Lady of Loretto in Dublin, whose Rule is inspired by St. Ignatius' *Spiritual Exercises*. The young woman learned that "man is created to praise, honor and serve God Our Lord, and thus save his own soul." Inspired by this principle, she wished "to help all men find the way to Heaven," beginning with the poorest of the poor.

She wanted to go to the missions, so she was sent to Darjeeling, in India, a city at the foot of the Himalayas, where she began her novitiate on May 24, 1929. Mother Teresa was a teacher and then the principal of this school for almost 20 years. In order to finish her studies she often had to go to Calcutta, and there she saw the unspeakably miserable conditions of the people who are born, live and die on the sidewalks. Often the babies die as soon as they are born and are immediately thrown into the trash or into a ditch. Every morning, the dead bodies are gathered up along with the garbage.

On September 10, 1946, while she was at prayer, Mother Teresa received her inspiration, her "call within a call." That day the thirst of Jesus' Heart for souls took possession of her heart, and this burning desire of the Savior became the foundation of her life. During the weeks and months that followed, Jesus revealed to her the desires of His Heart through interior visions.

He revealed to her how He suffers seeing the poorest of the poor simply abandoned to suffer and die, and how His Heart burns with the desire to be loved by them. Jesus asked Sr. Teresa to form a new religious community, called the Missionaries of Charity, dedicated to the service of the poorest of the poor.

For the first time, Sr. Teresa went to the poorest part of the city, visited the families, washed the children's wounds, and took care of the dying in the streets. She began each day with Mass and then went out into the filthiest parts of the city, Rosary in hand, to seek and serve Jesus in those who are "unwanted, unloved, and uncared-for."

Mother Teresa never asked for money, and she never owned any. Yet her works and foundations always needed large amounts of money. Divine Providence always saw to her needs, and Mother Teresa let herself be guided only by the needs of the poor.

From Mother Teresa's writings we can see that she had a deep devotion to Our Blessed Mother: "Mary is our guide, the cause of our joy. Pray to her. Say the Rosary so that Our Lady will always be with you, protect and help you. Start praying as a family. The family that prays together stays together."

St. Gianna Beretta Molla (1922-1962)
Doctor, Wife and Mother

St. Gianna Beretta Molla chose death rather than risk the life of the child in her womb

Gianna was born in Magenta, near Milan, into a deeply Christian family. She was the tenth of thirteen children, five of whom died in childhood and three of whom consecrated themselves to God.

Gianna received her First Communion when she was only five and a half, and from that day on she went to Mass every morning with her mother. Holy Communion became her indispensable daily food. Two years later, she received Confirmation.

At sixteen, at the end of a retreat, she wrote: "I want to fear mortal sin like a snake; it is a thousand times better to die than to offend the Lord."

During her life she underwent many physical and spiritual trials, which she bore courageously thanks to her strong faith. One of her school friends wrote of her: "Gianna gave us her sweet and calm smile, a reflection of her serene joy and peaceful soul."

After earning her medical degree, specializing in pediatrics, Gianna married the engineer Pietro Molla, hoping to have a large family. She soon had three children, but while she was expecting the fourth she became aware of a serious medical condition which threatened her own life and that of her child. She said to the surgeon who was to operate on her, "Don't worry about me; just take care of my baby." Later she added, "If you have to decide between me and the baby, don't hesitate: choose the child—I demand it—save him!"

After the birth of a healthy baby girl (who is alive today and is a doctor like her mother), Gianna suffered atrocious pain for a week. She died, saying, "Jesus, I love You! Jesus, I love You!"

While her cause for beatification was proceeding, overseen at first by then-Cardinal Archbishop of Milan, Giovanni Battista Montini, who later became Pope Paul VI, the first miracle took place—the healing of a gravely ill Brazilian mother. Some years later another miracle took place, again the healing of a mother in Brazil, this time one who was four months pregnant. On May 16, 2004, Gianna was canonized in the presence of her family.

The sacrifice of Gianna Beretta Molla continues to bear fruit!